HIDDEN TREASURES

Hidden Treasures
A 32-Day Devotional Filled with Psalms, Hymns, and Spiritual Songs

Copyright © 2025 Leah Harris

All rights reserved. No part of this publication may be reproduced in a retrieval system, or transmitted in any form or by any means—electronic, mechanical, photocopying, recording, or otherwise—without the prior written permission of the publisher.

While precaution has been taken in the preparation of this book, the publisher and author assume no responsibility for errors or omissions, or for damages resulting from the use of the information contained herein.

This book is set in the typeface *Athelas* designed by Veronika Burian and Jose Scaglione.

Paperback ISBN: 978-1-967262-03-8

A Publication of *Tall Pine Books*
PO Box 42 Warsaw | Indiana 46581
www.tallpinebooks.com

| 1 25 25 20 16 02 |

Published in the United States of America

HIDDEN TREASURES

A 32-Day Devotional Filled with
Psalms, Hymns, *and* Spiritual Songs

LEAH HARRIS

DEDICATION

To my beloved Savior, my Love, and my Friend. Thank You for all that You are. I pray this is pleasing to Your heart. To my husband, you are an amazing partner and a picture of Christ's love for the Church. Thank you for sowing into so many of my dreams. To our precious children, you are such a gift and the sunshine in our days. To our well-trained and highly intelligent dogs, we love you. Thank you to my daddy for never giving up on me: You hold a very special part of my heart. I miss you. May God abundantly bless all who have sown into my walk with Jesus over the years and who continue to help me grow in Christ.

Contents

Preface: How to Interact with this Devotional 9
Introduction: A Prayer and My Heart Cry 11

1. Divine Inspiration 13
2. Candlelight Dinner for Two: A Song in Heaven 15
3. God of All 19
4. My Love for You Is True 21
5. The One and Only 23
6. Prophetic Word for the Body 27
7. Prophetic Worship Song: There Is No Striving 29
8. Chandelier 33
9. Awaken to the Dreams of Your Heart 35
10. I Will Wait for You 37
11. The Way, the Truth, and the Life 39
12. The Power in the BLOOD of JESUS 43
13. Intimacy 45
14. A Song: We Will Be Ready for Our Bridegroom 47
15. A Word for the Body 51
16. Rest 53

17. You are Close	55
18. Becoming the Bride	57
19. Inheritance	59
20. A Song: My Sweet and Tender Gardener	61
21. Praise and Thanksgiving	65
22. Joy Comes in the Morning	67
23. Prophetic Worship: Come, Sit at My Feet	69
24. Legacy	71
25. Immanuel: A Song	73
26. Free	75
27. Trusting the Mighty One	77
28. The Day of the Lord	79
29. Anchor	81
30. Prophetic Word for the Body	83
31. Prophetic Worship: Good Morning, Beautiful	85
32. His Shalom Peace	87
In Closing	89
About the Author	93

PREFACE

How to Interact with this Devotional

This is not your typical devotional in that it has songs, poems, and psalms. One might wonder how to experience this devotional to the fullest. Here are a couple of suggestions that may be helpful.

- Reading out loud over yourself: Our bodies and minds respond to words we speak over ourselves and hearing it can sometimes be more impactful.
- Reading out loud to God as if you were reading a letter.
- Taking a "Selah" moment, like prefaced so often in the Psalms, to stop and pause in reflection of what you have read.
- Although there are no specific melodies given for the songs written, when something comes to your mind

and heart, sing it out loud in praise to the Lord! It does not have to sound like anything but your heart praising a worthy God!
- Be free and open to encounter God in this devotional however you are moved in your heart! You may find yourself inspired to write, draw, paint, dance, or make music! Be encouraged in the exploration and discovery of who you are in Jesus and let loose!
- There is no right or wrong way! Be blessed in your discovery of Him!

INTRODUCTION

A Prayer and My Heart Cry

The holy and only God! What worthy sentiments might I utter to my King? God, in His goodness, looks upon man's heart. How do I spill my heart out onto paper in a way that does Your beauty any justice? Help me discover the words, God. Guide and inspire me in creating the romance of our dance into a story that breathes Your life onto a page. What a beautiful way to live. Our secret place is the nearest and dearest chamber of my existence. It has been kept away from the world. And now, we desire to share it. I feel led to allow the light of Your countenance to shine for others into the brightest, fullest, deepest, sweetest place I have ever been. Our secret place—our secret space outside of time—where we meet face to face and discover one another in unity, eternally. This is an impartation to the nations of the most valuable treasure there ever has been or will be: knowing Christ the King intimately, our precious Jesus. That we might know Him and be known by Him.

So use the key of your heart to unlock your secret passageway. Go down the corridor into your sacred place and patiently await His Majesty. He is faithful to meet you there, to complete you there, if you dare. Have courage and take the leap of faith. Freefall into His love. Seek and you shall find all and immeasurably more than you have ever dreamed or sought for! Be blessed in your seeking and finding of Him.

I pray that in the encounter of His Spirit through this devotional, you experience an impartation of intimacy in your relationship with God. My hope is that He will awaken your heart and unveil your senses to perceive Him in ways you have never imagined. Enjoy! God, prepare hearts to receive!

DAY 1

Divine Inspiration

"He that believeth on Me, as the Scriptures have said, out of his belly will flow rivers of living water." (John 7:38)

"Ask and it will be given to you; seek and you will find; knock and the door will be opened to you." (Matthew 7:7)

Poetry is like the ocean. It flows in a rhythmic motion, as does the hypnotic lull of the seas. Words sway back and forth, twisting and turning—creating and forming a story, one sentence at a time.

Divine inspiration often comes in like the tide, bubbling up as waves of glory, crashing over us in our intimate time.

Sometimes it can seem violent, like a hurricane of commotion—encountering us in a whirlwind of emotion.

Divine inspiration might appear as a calm day at sea—with words—like a message in a bottle floating up to you or to me.

Sometimes His words seem to want to be found. They lie as buried treasure, eager to be discovered in the depths of intimacy.

That feels like poetry to me. It is a dance, a romance with words moving in a fluid motion, interacting with one another in a beautiful image of unity.

Together they form sentences, shape a picture, paint a dream, and cast a vision through colorful phrases—marking a moment in time shared through the weaving of a story mapping the colors of one's heart for all the world to see.

It is a declaration of bravery. I have boldly decided to share something that has come from the depths of me—from the rivers—from the oceans—the seas flowing in motion—within my belly.

Just as I was created to be—twisting, shaping, and forming a story with my King—from the purest place of *into—Him—I—see*. My heart confessed onto paper, to be shared by what started as a moment in time—a minuscule wave in the sea; a thought or a ponder; a walk or a wander.

So just sit and wonder—"What is the story stirring inside of me?"

> **QUESTION OF THE DAY:** *What is the creative story stirring inside of you? Is there something creative that you have always wanted to do?*

DAY 2

Candlelight Dinner for Two: A Song in Heaven

"Behold, I stand at the door, and knock; if any man hear My voice, and open the door, I will come in to him, and will sup with him, and he with Me." (Revelation 3:20)

INTRO

Candlelight dinner for two.
Just for me and for you.
The Bride and her Groom.
The King and His Queen.
Come in and sup with me.
At this table prepared before thee.
For I am Yours, and You are mine.
Candlelight for two.

VERSE 1

Oh, my dear King, after my own heart! You are all that I need.
I am she who came out from the wilderness leaning on her beloved!
You redeemed my life from the pit and crowned me with love and kindness!
You have adorned me in the finest garments and most precious jewels.
I will forever love you with all my heart, with all my soul, and with all my strength!
So come in, my King, and sup with me.

CHORUS

Candlelight dinner for two.
Just for me and for you.
The Bride and her Groom.
The King and His Queen.
Come in and sup with me.
At this table prepared before thee.
For I am Yours, and You are mine.
Candlelight for two.

VERSE 2

Come dine with me in our secret place, for I seek Your face.

Where every chamber in my heart has been made ready for You!

I am a Bride, prepared for her King, made perfect without spot or blemish.

In purity, I long for thee, awaiting our royal wedding.

My life is my reasonable offering and I pour it out at Your feet.

So come in, my King, and sup with me.

CHORUS

Candlelight dinner for two.
Just for me and for you.
The Bride and her Groom.
The King and His Queen.
Come in and sup with me.
At this table prepared before thee.
For I am Yours, and You are mine.
Candlelight for two.

VERSE 3

All of my fountains are in You, and You are all that satisfies.

As a deer pants for streams of water, so my soul thirsts after You!

Come quench my thirst and fill my hunger with Your living bread of truth!

You have set a table before me, and now I beckon for You to join me.
I am recklessly devoted to You, and my heart's desires are in You.
So come in, my King, and sup with me.

CHORUS

Candlelight dinner for two.
Just for me and for you.
The Bride and her Groom.
The King and His Queen.
Come in and sup with me.
At this table prepared before thee.
For I am Yours, and You are mine.
Candlelight for two.

OUTRO

So, come in, sweet King, and sup with me. Come be with me eternally.
For we will never part! No, we will never part.

QUESTION OF THE DAY: *Plan out a date with God where you can spend time with Him, kind of like you would for a spouse or close friend. What would it look like?*

DAY 3

God of All

"He has made everything beautiful in its time. Also, He has put eternity into man's heart, yet so that he cannot find out what God has done from the beginning to the end." (Ecclesiastes 3:11)

I love You, God of all,
You are everything to me,
Every tear, every smile,
Every hurt, every joy,
Every moment of humility,
Every moment of serenity,
The east and the west,
The north and the south,
The shore and the tide,
The vastness of the ocean.
The narrow path of the river,
The depths of the canyon,
The darkness of the cavern,

Everything mirrors You,
The beauty of Your creation,
The touch of Your hand,
The life You have given all,
Bringing me closer to You,
And closer into Eternity,
Already alive in me,
I love You, God of all

QUESTION OF THE DAY: *What areas of life not mentioned here do you see God in? Big and small?*

DAY 4

My Love for You Is True

"Love the Lord your God with all your heart, with all your soul, with all your strength, and with all your mind, and love your neighbor as yourself." (Luke 10:27)

"The Lord does not look at the things people look at. People look at the outward appearance, but the Lord looks at the heart." (1 Samuel 16:7)

"And whatever you do, whether in word or deed, do it all in the name of the Lord Jesus, giving thanks to God the Father through Him."(Colossians 3:17)

I love You, with all of my heart, my soul, my strength, and my mind.
My deepest desires are for You.
You have hidden me in the cleft of the rock.
I am set apart, consecrated for the Holy One.
God, how can I show You? What could I say? What could I do? Look upon my heart, and know me—the depth of my love for You!

Agape Love—the deepest of deep waters, and I pray that You would deepen my love for You still!
I hear You saying this is just the beginning.
My heart is singing a song of hope and restoration!
A sweet melody as You dance joyfully over me.
What kind of God is this—that He would love us so?
Give me words, for out of the mouth, the abundance of the heart speaks. So give me truths to utter, to make my heart known for You.
What a beautiful romance,
A love so sweet and pure,
Yet violent in its sacrifice,
Oh, to know this God and to love Him,
What else is there but Your face?
So, look upon my heart and know me—the depth of my love for You!
In all that I am and in all that I will do, my heart does unto You.

QUESTION OF THE DAY: *How does God show you personally how much He loves you? Write a small poem or "thank you" to Him for this!*

DAY 5

The One and Only

"Who is like the Lord Our God, Who dwells on high, Who humbles Himself to behold things that are in the heavens and in the earth? He raises the poor out of the dust. And lifts the needy out of the ash heap, that He may seat him with princes—With the princes of His people. He grants the barren woman a home, Like a joyful mother of children." (Psalm 113:5-9)

With the spirit of the world stirring around me;
In the chaos of all that spins in turmoil—
I stand still.
I see this deception as a fog. It is swirling—moving—creating smoke and mirrors—devouring peace by keeping people in disillusionment.
Though grieved by what I see, my heart is still.
I hear You beckoning me with a gentle whisper.
My heart sounds like a drum's beat;

In perfect rhythm with the move of Your Spirit.
I feel the wind upon my cheek, and yet I remain still.
Listening. I turn away from the distractions. Then, I cry out to You!
Draw me out into the dark and still of the night—the quiet of nothing around me—just us.
The darkness is as light to You, and Your light is all I need.
Come, and be with me in this place.
Away from the spinning of the world's cares and its worries—
That we might weave our own story to clothe me with.
Let us search for secrets in each other's eyes.
Like brand-new lovers, with so much to discover.
Enamored with each joyous surprise.
Let us write about our love's story.
About You and me.
A child-like tale of epic romance.
You are valiantly here to rescue the damsel who was distressed.
You have captured my attention, eternally.
All of my affections are Yours,
All of my fountains are in You,
My gaze has left the things of this world,
Clinging to your eyes.
The brilliance of Your light is drawing me further and ever further away.

Until the world feels like a very distant memory outside of time and space.

I have followed You out into the dark of the night—the wilderness—

With only Your light to guide me and Your Spirit to sustain my life.

I am mesmerized by Your beauty,

In You, I find the provision of all I need.

QUESTION OF THE DAY: *What have you left behind in the world to turn and walk with God? Thank Him for this freedom and focus on His face!*

DAY 6

Prophetic Word for the Body

"Behold, I am doing a new thing; now it springs forth, do you not perceive it? I will make a way in the wilderness and rivers in the desert." (Isaiah 43:19)

"Be strong and courageous. Do not be afraid or terrified because of them, for the Lord your God goes with you; He will never leave nor forsake you." (Deuteronomy 31:6)

I am giving My people direction today. Although for a time, some have felt as if they were aimlessly blowing in the wind, today, the compass stops spinning and points in the direction you should go! You have heard the clock ticking in the natural and it has made you in a hurry to move at the world's pace. But today, cease your striving. For the things of the Spirit move in My Eternal time frame, and I am in no hurry, beloved. My timing is perfect. The rest and appointed times of God are coming upon you in the true peace of My Spirit. I am teaching you to wait upon Me and build your faith in this place.

This season has been a time of preparation, and now your bags are full and your journey is laid out before you. I have gone ahead of you, clearing the way through the debris of confusion and tempering the fires of longsuffering. Remember this day as I say that even when there seems not to be a way, I have made a way for you! So take flight, beloved. Be on your way. I will be with you! And be expectant. For the grass is greener in the days marked ahead. Take joy in the journey and remember to keep your eyes looking up!

QUESTION OF THE DAY: *Ask God what new thing He is doing or wants to do in your heart, life, family, work, or finances.*

DAY 7

Prophetic Worship Song: There Is No Striving

"Cease striving and know that I am God." (Psalm 46:10)

"The steadfast love of the Lord never ceases, His mercies never come to an end; They are new every morning; Great is Your faithfulness." (Lamentations 3:22-23)

*Suggestion: Read this song out loud as worship to God or sing it to Him and over yourself.

In You my soul finds rest. Oh, in You my soul finds rest. No more striving in the Beloved. For you are already loved in Christ Jesus. So, sit and rest, My child. Oh, come and rest your weary head. In You, my soul finds rest. In You, my soul finds rest. There is no striving in the Beloved. You are already made perfect, you are already loved. So, come and lay your weary head. Yes, come and lay your weary head. There is no striving in Me, My child. There is no striving to be My child.

Oh, do you not know that you are already good enough? Do you not know that you are already made perfect in My love? Come and rest your weary head. Because there is no striving, there is no striving in My love. You are already made perfect in Me, My child. So, come lay, come lay your weary head. There is no striving in My love. You are already enough, made perfect in My love. Come and lay your weary head because there is no striving, and you are already good enough. Come and lay your weary head. Because there is no striving in My love. You are already good enough. Perfected in My Blood. There is no striving, My child. So, come lay your weary head. It's time for bed. Come and sleep in the stern of My heart. No matter the storm. No matter the wind. Do not be frightened, little child. For I have overcome the wicked one. There is no striving. Come and rest. Oh, you are already perfected in My love. Come and lay your weary head. Because there is no striving, there is no striving, there is no need to strive. Oh, you are already good enough. There is no striving, there is no striving. My love was a gift. You cannot earn that which is given freely. Yes, my Son was a gift and you cannot earn it. So, come and lay your weary head. Cause there is no striving, there is no striving. Yeah, my Son was a gift and you cannot earn that which is given freely. No, so come and rest your weary head. My Son was a gift and you cannot earn it. So, come and rest your weary head; there is no striving in the Beloved. Oh, my Son was a gift. You cannot earn it. So, come and lay your head in the stern of My heart and rest. Oh, come and rest, My beloved child. You are no longer under the law of sin and death. You are resurrected in abundant life. So, don't think twice, just come and rest. Lay your head down. Enjoy the view. As I sing over you, My child. You cannot earn that which is given freely. My Son was a gift, so enjoy that which is given to you. Yeah, enjoy abundant life. Come and rest in My love. I said, come and rest in My love. Oh, come and rest in My love. In a bed of roses made for you. Set apart in pure love in the blood of Jesus. Oh, lay your head down. Come and rest. You cannot earn that which is given freely. From Me to you. So, come and rest.

QUESTION OF THE DAY: *What areas of your life is God calling you to rest and surrender to Him in? How can you rest in the finished works of Jesus and His sacrifice more?*

DAY 8

Chandelier

"You are the light of the world. A town built on a hill cannot be hidden." (Matthew 5:14)

No mixture,
I see a light fixture,
With no mixture,
Just pure, white light,
God sent His light,
To shine so bright,
No shift or shadow,
With no mixture,
Painting a picture,
His spotless Bride,
For whom He died,
He suffered,
A spear in His side,
For her, all dressed in white,
Dazzling prisms.

Free of life's schisms,
Shining His Truth,
In unity,
In humble beauty,
No mixture,
No restraints,
No constraints,
No distortions,
Pure prisms of every color,
Shining shamelessly,
Blamelessly,
All in His glory,
All for His story,
Rainbow prisms of promises,
Lighting up the world,
The Shining Body of Christ.

QUESTION OF THE DAY: *How has God purified you as His Bride? Thank Him for these victories and humbly ask for more!*

DAY 9

Awaken to the Dreams of Your Heart

"'For I know the plans I have for you,' declares the Lord, 'plans to prosper you and not to harm you, plans to give you hope and a future. Then you will call on Me and come and pray to Me, and I will listen to you.'" (Jeremiah 29:11-12)

A dream is awakened in the middle of the night.
Inspired, it floated from dark depths into light.
It had waited until the timing was right.
The timing is now, and it rose quickly into sight.
Breathe on this dream!
Give it wings for flight!
It will take courage and sacrifice!
But, it was born for the sky, and it is worth the fight!
Do not be afraid. Pursue its destiny with all your might.
There is no failure—the goal is only to set your heart alight!

An on-fire vision.

A passionate heart.

Sailing dreams on His winds of freedom.

Flying free as a kite.

Do not hesitate!

The time is now.

Shout, "Awaken!" to the dreams of your heart!

QUESTION OF THE DAY: *What dreams do you feel are stirring in your heart? How can you pursue them with God by your side?*

DAY 10

I Will Wait for You

"Wait for the Lord; Be strong, and let your heart take courage; Yes, wait for the Lord." (Psalm 27:14)

I will wait for You as the sky awaits the sun to rise.
I will wait for You as the field awaits the flower's bloom.
I will wait for You as the birds await their young to fly.
I will wait for You.
For Your timing is always perfect.
Your promises are always true.
All of my fountains are in You.
I move to the drum of Your heart's beat.
I will not miss a step by Your leading.
And so I wait for You.
Patiently I wait.
Trusting that in the waiting, You are building my faith.

I will wait for You like the shore awaits the water's rise.
I will wait for You as the moon awaits the late-night tide.

I will wait for You as the desert awaits the latter rain.
I will wait for You as a mother awaits her child's birth.
I will wait for You.
For Your timing is always perfect.
Your promises are always true.
All of my fountains are in You.
I move to the drum of Your heart's beat.
I will not miss a step of Your leading.
And so I wait for You.
Patiently I will wait.
Trusting that in the waiting, You are building my faith.

QUESTION OF THE DAY: *Are there promises from God that you have had to be patient and wait on? What are they? How could you partner with God while waiting for these promises to be fulfilled? Write down your thoughts.*

DAY 11

The Way, the Truth, and the Life

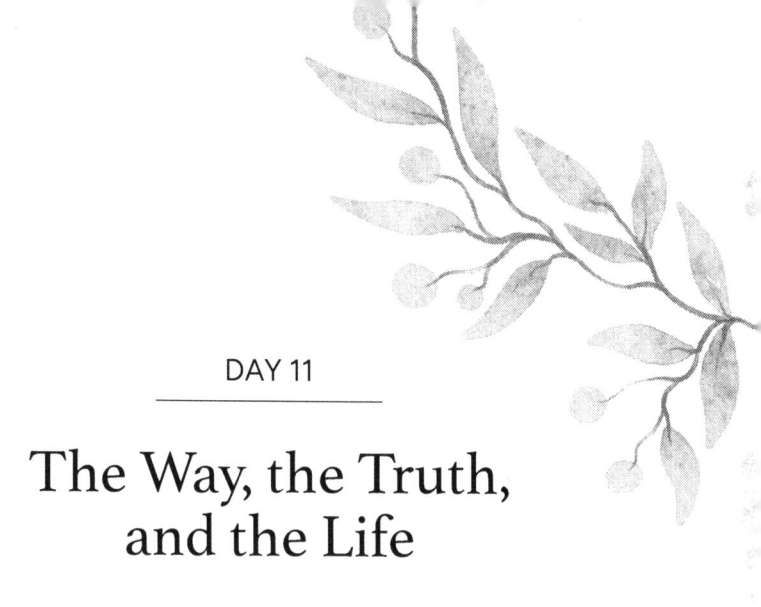

"Jesus said to him, 'I am the way, the truth, and the life. No one comes to the Father except through Me.'" (John 14:6)

VERSE 1

Take my hand and lead me.
Past the road most traveled.
It is the narrow gate I seek.
Depart! All this world!
For He has made a way for me.

CHORUS

What else is there but Your face?
What else is there but Your warm embrace?
Depart! All of this world!
It is my Lover's face I seek.

Face to face and cheek to cheek.
We will dance through eternity.

VERSE 2

Take my heart and keep me.
You are the keeper of the keep.
Purified and set apart.
A Bride made holy unto Thee.
Depart! All this world.
It is the purest truth I seek.

CHORUS

What else is there but Your face?
What else is there but Your warm embrace?
Depart! All of this world!
It is my Lover's face I seek.

VERSE 3

Take my life and read me.
Like an open book.
Every page unto You.
No matter what it took.
So depart! All this world.
A life written by His hands.

CHORUS

What else is there but Your face?
What else is there but Your warm embrace?
Depart! All of this world!
It is my Lover's face I seek.
Face to face and cheek to cheek.
We will dance through eternity.

QUESTION OF THE DAY: *How has God directed your life by showing you the way, sustaining you through His life, and giving you His truth?*

DAY 12

The Power in the BLOOD of JESUS

"The Lord is King for ever and ever; the nations will perish from His land. You, Lord, hear the desire of the afflicted; You encourage them, and You listen to their cry, defending the fatherless and the oppressed, so that mere earthly mortals will never again strike terror." (Psalm 10: 16-18)

I am me again! I am Your Beloved child! The me that You created and knew from the beginning! As I look in the mirror, I barely recognize myself. "Who is she coming out of the wilderness, leaning on her Beloved?" What magnificent work You have done within me. The creative wonder of Your hand. The Potter reforming the mired clay into His masterpiece; Your beauty from my ashes. Now I see the reflection of Your Son, and my heart spills tears of joy. I am me again. I am Your daughter! I am Your precious child; I am what You intended when You set Your heart to creating me. So tenderly You thought over my existence, brooding as a hen over her eggs.

Just as You hovered over the waters in the beginning! Sitting on ideas and creative imaginings of who I would become. You spent Your time forming me in the womb. So fearfully and wonderfully made am I. Though for a time I was lost, I have been found! What amazing grace! In Your deep patience and yearning after me, You waited until the timing was right to bring me back to You! What a miraculous story of love and the miracle of its redemptive power! Thank You, God, for all that You are! It is breathtaking. You have continually restored to me all that was lost or stolen. You have made all things beautiful in Your time, and I am a new creation in Christ Jesus! Bless Your holy name! My whole heart sings a song of praise to my God! You are everything! You are lovely, and I am lovely because I am Yours. I am in You and You are in me! "Abide in the vine, and you will bear much fruit!"

QUESTION OF THE DAY: *How has God restored your life? Thank God for the ways He has restored you. Write a couple of the ways He has made you new.*

DAY 13

Intimacy

"It is the glory of God to conceal things; but the glory of kings is to search things out." (Proverbs 25:2)

"Awake, O harp and lyre! I will awaken the dawn!" (Psalm 108:2)

"Oh Lord, in the morning You hear my voice; in the morning I prepare a sacrifice for You and watch." (Psalm 5:3)

Silence the soul,
Shhh…ever so quietly,
Listen in, Deeper,
Deeper, Longer still,
In the ending of the night,
The early hours of the morning,
The sun's first breath,
Before dawn's first light,
Stay and wait in this place.
Awaiting the glorious light

The Son's light of revelation.
As the dawning sun, it warms the day.
Bringing forth new life.
Dive into the wonders of God.
As they unfold,
Ancient mysteries before history,
Yet they remain untold,
Divine treasures, buried for such a time,
Deep within the heart of God.
What a beautiful love story,
Me chasing after You,
While You chase after me.
Unlock the pearly white gates of my heart,
As I seek out the deepest crevices of WHO YOU ARE.
Revealed; unveiled; beauty; majesty,
A miraculous encounter,
An eternal endeavor,
A lifelong adventure,
Beginning each day,
The freshness of the morning,
As I await Your coming,
Looking upon the Face of Glory,
BEHOLD.

QUESTION OF THE DAY: *What are some ways you could intentionally become more still before the Lord? Make a plan and follow through.*

DAY 14

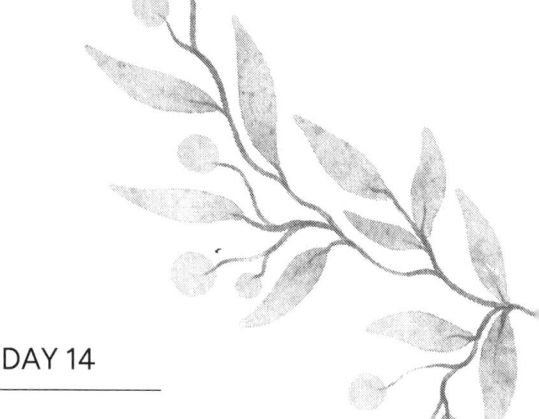

A Song: We Will Be Ready for Our Bridegroom

"The battle is not yours, but God's."(2 Chronicles 20:1-29)

"Enoch, the seventh from Adam, prophesied about them: 'See, the Lord is coming with thousands upon thousands of His holy ones to judge everyone, and to convict all of them of all the ungodly acts they have committed in their ungodliness, and of all the defiant words ungodly sinners have spoken against Him.'" (Jude 1:14-15)

VERSE 1

    Mighty men of valor.
    Righteous women of power.
    Step into the light.
    Step into the fight.
    For the battle is the Lord's.
    And the blood's been sacrificed.

CHORUS

>Jesus is coming back soon.
>We'll be ready for the Bridegroom.
>We'll be ready for our Bridegroom.
>Jesus is coming back soon.
>We'll be ready for the Bridegroom.
>We'll be ready for our Bridegroom.

VERSE 2

>Come holy fire and rain.
>Burn up all the chaff.
>Wash us with Your cleansing Word.
>The old man has been crucified.
>Your resurrection has brought new life.
>The old has passed away; the new has come.

CHORUS

>Jesus is coming back soon.
>We'll be ready for the Bridegroom.
>We'll be ready for our Bridegroom.
>Jesus is coming back soon.
>We'll be ready for the Bridegroom.
>We'll be ready for our Bridegroom.

VERSE 3

Awaken, Remnant Bride.
Rise, warriors, rise.
This is our war cry.
Dry bones, come alive!
Step into your rightful place.
As joint heirs to the throne of grace!

CHORUS

Jesus is coming back soon.
We'll be ready for the Bridegroom.
We'll be ready for our Bridegroom.
Jesus is coming back soon.
We'll be ready for the Bridegroom.
We'll be ready for our Bridegroom.

QUESTION OF THE DAY: *How are you preparing for the King's coming?*

DAY 15

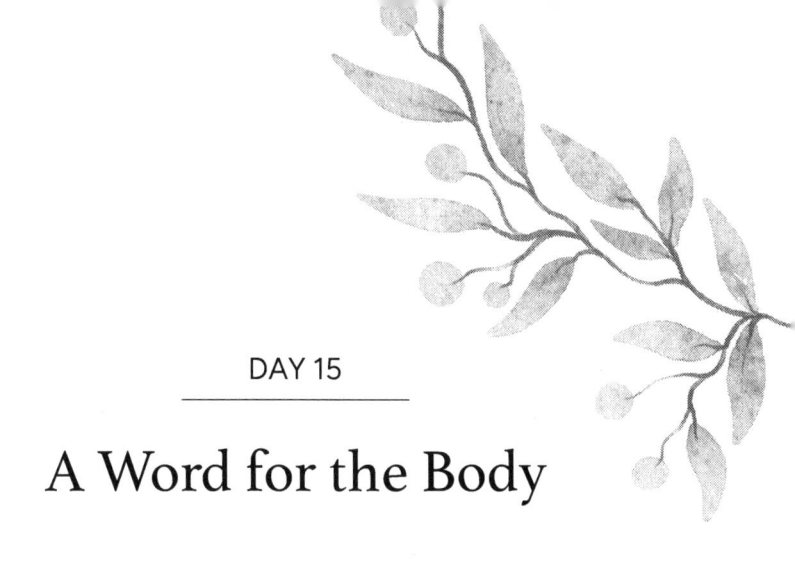

A Word for the Body

"The thief comes only to steal, kill, and destroy; I have come that they may have life, and have it more abundantly." (John 10:10)

"Then Jesus declared, 'I am the bread of life. Whoever comes to Me will never go hungry, and whoever believes in Me will never be thirsty.'" (John 6:35)

Get ready! I am coming full speed ahead. I am blowing in like a strong wind on a quiet day and stirring things up! In the Spirit and in your lives! "Awake north wind, and come, south wind! Blow on my garden, that its fragrance may spread everywhere. Let my beloved come into his garden and taste its choice fruits!" God is bringing the breath of His Spirit to blow upon the gardens of His people and stir up the fragrance and aroma of Christ! He is looking upon the fruit of a bountiful harvest to come. Abide in the vine, and you will bear much fruit! John 15:7 says, "If you abide in me, and my words abide in you, you shall ask whatever you wish, and to you it will come to pass."

Hang onto Me tightly, and the world around you loosely. Everything that can be shaken will be shaken in this time of pruning and burning of the old. I am purifying My Bride, and adorning her with new jewels and wedding garments! For I come for a Bride that has eyes for only Me! Do not fall into the trap of a double-minded heart and lukewarm affection. The gate is narrow, beloved, and only the necessary provision will be accepted! Feast on My flesh and drink My Blood! Every other fountain will run dry as you realize that I alone am the source of life! Every other source is vanity (vapor) and will not last! My Word is eternal. Cling to Me and receive life and life more abundantly.

QUESTION OF THE DAY: *In what ways can you trust God more, and how can you put that into practice? Pray and write down one to three action steps that come to your mind.*

DAY 16

Rest

"And He shall be their peace." (Micah 5:5)

"Who the Son sets free is free indeed." (John 8:36)

I REST in Your unfailing grace.
My heart is still in this safe place.
On You I lean, fixed on Your face.
What love, what love, my past erased.
Oh, the delight of Your yoke upon me.
The bliss of Your presence rests on me.
This is Your perfect will for me.
Our precious exchange of intimacy.
What love, what love—This wonder amazes me.
What love, what love—His love sets me free.
Continually! A perpetual state of freedom and more freedom.
Forever I increase the span of my wings.
Because of what Jesus has done for me.
Taking more and more territory.

I claim HIS victory with the authority given to me in this place called REST.

QUESTION OF THE DAY: *In what ways has God set you free through His Love and given you rest within your life? Thank God for these ways and celebrate!*

DAY 17

You are Close

"*Call to Me and I will answer you and show you great and mighty things you do not know.*" (Jeremiah 33:3)

"*Draw near to God and He will draw near to you.*" (James 4:8)

You are not so far.
You are not so far away.
You are not so far away from me.
That I could not see Your face.
For as I have called to You.
Drawing near to You in the depth of my heart.
You have answered me.
You have drawn near to me.
Drawing me into the dearest part of Your heart.
Showing me great and mighty things I did not know.
You are not so far.
You are not so far away.
You are not so far away from me.

Instead, You are drawing ever closer into me.
I hear You so clearly.
As You speak, my spirit listens to perceive.
Sweet somethings that are special and unique.
Specifically uttered from Your heart for mine to receive.
No, You are not so far.
You have never been so far away.
That I could not have reached out and touched Your face.
You have chosen to abide inside of me.
Dwelling within me by the work of Your Holy Spirit.
So graciously, You speak to me
Reminding me that You will always be near
You will never leave nor forsake me
You have chosen to draw near—eternally
As the depths of my heart draw near to You.

QUESTION OF THE DAY: *In what ways have you felt far from God? Take a second to talk about those things with Him. Then invite the Holy Spirit to invade those places in your heart and life!*

DAY 18

Becoming the Bride

"He who dwells in the Shelter of the Most High will rest in the Shadow of the Almighty. I will say of the Lord, He is my Refuge and Fortress, my God in whom I trust." Psalm 91:1-2

Your love for me is so tender and so sweet
You come to me so gentle and so meek
Depart! All this world
It is my Lover's face I seek
The One who keeps me so perfectly
Beneath the shadow of His wings
No harm will come to me
I am at rest within the peaceful arms of my Beloved
Oh, what a love story
What a testimony to His glory
A story filled with wonder that is pure love
It is tangible
It is real
Yet, furiously surreal

It mends the wounded and heals the brokenhearted
Yes, this story is written specifically for me
A personal tale of victory for each child of history
Christ died for us all
The Son rose for the wicked and the righteous
Oh, to know You and to be known by You
How can it be
This love that has captured me
The Romancer enrapturing me—in a bed of pure love
A garden of divine roses with the sweetest of aromas
The majestic aroma of Christ's sacrifice
Upon a cross. He paid the price for me
And now my head rests upon His chest
I am entangled fully in His beauty
In Him, my love has come undone

QUESTION OF THE DAY: *What do you enjoy about your relationship with God? Spend a few moments telling God how much you enjoy those aspects of your relationship with Him.*

DAY 19

Inheritance

"Sing and rejoice, O Daughter of Zion! For behold, I come, and dwell in the midst of you, says the Lord." (Zephaniah 2:10)

"Incline Your ear to me; rescue me speedily! Be a rock of refuge for me, a strong fortress to save me!" (Psalm 31:2)

I love You, God.
Do not let the world steal what You have rightfully purchased on the cross.
Our precious time getting to know each other, in relationship.
Oh, to walk with You in the cool of the evening.
Enjoying the simplicity of Your company.
Hand in hand, side by side, stride in stride.
This is where my heart longs to be.
Within the Eternal One.
The One who was and is and is to come.
The One who has known me from the beginning.

He is not surprised by my flaws, my weaknesses, my struggles.

Even in the darkest night, He is singing a beautiful melody over me.

He meets me there, for darkness is as light to Him.

No, He is not ashamed to call me His own.

Instead, He shows Himself mighty on my behalf.

Charging in on a cloud in all of His glory.

My white knight on His white horse who comes to save me.

Time and time again, He is faithful.

He is my rescue and my defense.

His strength made perfect in my weakness.

Behold! The glory of my King as He comes to rescue me.

QUESTION OF THE DAY: *What promises do you sense God has made to you personally? Thank Him and claim these promises as part of your inheritance from the Lord!*

DAY 20

A Song: My Sweet and Tender Gardener

"A garden enclosed is my sister, my spouse; a spring shut up, a fountain sealed. Thy plants are an orchard of pomegranates, with pleasant fruits; camphire, with spikenard, and saffron; calamus and cinnamon, with all trees of frankincense; myrrh and aloes, with all the chief spices: A fountain of gardens, a well of living waters, and streams from Lebanon." (Songs of Songs 4:12-15)

CHORUS

> You are all that I need.
> My love, my dove, my dear one.
> It is You I desire to please.
> My love, my dove, my near one. So, come, my sweet King.
> Tend the gardens of my heart.
> Pull up any root that is displeasing to You!
> Oh, come, my sweet King!
> Tend the gardens of my heart.

VERSE 1

My sweet and tender Gardener.
So diligently You keep the plow.
Tilling the depth of the soil by day.
Guarding the vineyards by night.
Plant the seeds of Your Word within me.
That I may flourish as a mighty oak tree.

CHORUS

You are all that I need.
My love, my dove, my dear one.
It is You I desire to please.
My love, my dove, my near one. So, come, my sweet King.
Tend the gardens of my heart.
Pull up any root that is displeasing to You!
Oh, come, my sweet King!
Tend the gardens of my heart.

VERSE 2

Let the winds blow upon my garden.
Stir up the spices that are pleasing.
May the blossoms saturate the air!
Drawing multitudes by a fragrance so fair.
A bowl of incense for You is rising to You.
Be delighted, as You walk in my garden.
In the cool of the evening, I sing a sweet song to you.

CHORUS

You are all that I need.
My love, my dove, my dear one.
It is You I desire to please.
My love, my dove, my near one. So, come, my sweet King.
Tend the gardens of my heart.
Pull up any root that is displeasing to You!
Oh, come, my sweet King!
Tend the gardens of my heart.

VERSE 3

Upon this land, the harvest is plentiful.
Within this garden, the soil is pliable.
Within my heart, the spices are stirring.
Upon my life, His winds are blowing.
Igniting the world with the fragrance of His love.
Alight upon me in a fresh fire, my dove!

QUESTION OF THE DAY: *Lord, what part of my heart do You specifically want to work on? Whatever you feel Him tugging on or highlighting to you, submit that to Him as your Gardener and Lord.*

DAY 21

Praise and Thanksgiving

"Those who know Your name trust in You, for You, Lord, have never forsaken those who seek You." (Psalm 9:10)

Though I cannot see, I will trust You.
For if You are leading, am I supposed to know where I go?
I will follow You in a faithful walk of obedience.
To the ends of the earth.
To the bottom of the sea.
Up the highest peak of the mountain.
In the darkest valley's peak.
Into the experiential knowledge of Your love for me.
Though I cannot see, I will trust You.
For if I am following, what should I see as You lead?
I see Your faithfulness, my constant one.
I see Your comfort, my gentle dove.
I will follow the surety of Your promises to me.
I will follow the faithfulness of Your love to keep me.
Though I cannot see, I will trust You.

I will trust that You have been where I am going.
That You await me there and have also prepared the way.
I will not turn to the right or the left.
I will not hesitate to check the path behind me.
For I know the prosperity of Your hand over me.
That Your glory is my rearguard.
That You have made a clear path.
Yes, by Your fiery hand, You forged the path before me.
Your light will be a lamp unto my feet and a light unto my path.
Your statutes, Your law, Your words, they keep me.
Delivering me from the falsities of the enemy.
You are my strong tower! Into You I run and I am safe.

QUESTION OF THE DAY: *How have you grown in trusting God in the last year or so? In what areas can you trust God more?*

DAY 22

Joy Comes in the Morning

"Those who sow in tears will reap with songs of joy." (Psalm 126:5)

"For His anger lasts only a moment, but His favor lasts a lifetime; weeping may stay for the night, but rejoicing comes in the morning." (Psalm 30:5)

In the stillness of the night.
Yes, in the dark night of the soul.
A song springs forth.
A song! A song springs forth from my heart!
Singing, come awaken the dawn!
Come awaken the dawn!
Oh, harp and lyre!
In the stillness of the night.
In the dark night of the soul.
A song! A song! A song springs forth.
My heart speaks to the morning light!
Come awaken the dawn.

Yes, a song! A song! A song springs forth.
Beckoning the joy of morning. Awakening the beauty of a new day!

QUESTION OF THE DAY: *In what area of your life are you wanting to have more joy? Write it down and thank God for this joy being fulfilled in this area of your life. Ask God to put some action steps on your heart to intentionally create joy in this area of your life.*

DAY 23

Prophetic Worship: Come, Sit at My Feet

'Martha, Martha,' the Lord answered, 'You are worried and upset about many things, but few things are needed—or indeed only one. Mary has chosen what is better, and it will not be taken away from her.'" (Luke 10:41-42)

Won't you come and sit at My feet?
Won't you come just to be with Me?
For I delight in your company, My child.
I delight in your company, My child.
Won't you come just to be at My feet? Oh, come and be with Me.
For I delight in your company. Yes! I delight in your company.
I just want to get to know you. Like it was the first time.
I just want to get to know you.
Like it was the last time.
I just want to sit and talk with you like we used to.

Won't you come and sit at My feet?
Won't you come just to be with Me?
So, come, My child.
Come experience Me in a new way.
Let Me show you things.
It's a new day.
Before the sun awakens.
Child, come and sit at My feet.
Come! Just to be with Me.
Come and sit at My feet.
Beloved, I love your company.
My beloved, I love your company.

QUESTION OF THE DAY: *Think about ways you can spend more time communing with God and journal them here. Then, put it into action.*

DAY 24

Legacy

"Hope deferred makes the heart sick, but a promise fulfilled is a tree of life." (Proverbs 13:12)

"Fear not, little flock, for it is your Father's good pleasure to give you the kingdom." (Luke 12:32)

Thank You. Thank You. Thank You.
From the bottom of my heart.
From the depths of my soul.
In the intimate union of our spirits.
Thank You. Thank You. Thank You. I am lost for words to say.
I am in awe of You each new day.
Not because I did not know You to be capable of such great things.
But because I never saw how great my life would be.
I was used to blinders on the sides of my eyes.
Casting a vision, never looking to the left or the right.
Again, I have dreamt too small.

And again and again, You remind me.
"Dream big. Dream big. Dream big.
My child, My child, you can have it all!"
As I look out upon the meadows set before me.
I see Your hand expand, pointing across the horizon.
This is all that You have promised to me.
A width and distance, farther than my eyes can see.
Then You point to the stars and begin to name them.
More numerous than the stars will your descendants be.
For you will leave a legacy on this earth of My children.
And My children's children.
For generations and generations to come!
They will be known as "The Faithful Ones."

QUESTION OF THE DAY: *Write a thank you note to God for promises and prayers you have seen come to pass in your life! Praise Him for the inheritance granted to us in Christ Jesus.*

DAY 25

Immanuel: A Song

VERSE 1

When life starts to get me down.
My God comes running after me.
When the enemy sets a snare for my feet,
Here my God comes to deliver me!
He is my rock and my shield.
My God in whom I trust.
My strength and my fortress.
My answer when times get tough.
He is the mighty God of Israel,
And He never sleeps.
Even in the darkest night,
I will not fear, for my God is with me!
Immanuel, God with us.
Immanuel, God for us.
Immanuel, God in us.
Victory, eternally.

REPEAT VERSE 1

VERSE 2

So when life starts to get you down.
Your God comes running after you.
When the enemy sets a snare for your feet,
Here your God comes to deliver you.
Your rock and your shield.
Your God in whom you trust.
Your strength and your fortress.
Your answer when times get tough.
He is the mighty God of Israel.
And He never sleeps.
Yes! Even in the darkest nights.
You will not fear for your God is with you!
Immanuel, God with us.
Immanuel, God for us.
Immanuel, God in us.
Victory, eternally. (2)

QUESTION OF DAY: WHAT *does it truly mean to you that God is always with you, for you, and abiding in you?*

DAY 26

Free

"Even youths grow tired and weary, and young men stumble and fall, but those who hope in the Lord will renew their strength. They will soar on wings as eagles; they will run and not grow weary. They shall walk and not be faint." (Isaiah 40:30-31)

As an eagle flies.
As a bird sings.
As a poet writes.
As a dreamer dreams.
The purpose of God is being released.
We are as children, running wild and free!
In a mother's heart.
In a guitar's strings.
In the pride of a lion.
In the waves of the sea.
The purpose of God is being released.
We are as children, running wild and free!

At the depths of the ocean.
At the top of the peak.
In the length of the river.
In the span of an eagle's wings.
The purpose of God is being released.
We are as children, running wild and free!

QUESTION OF THE DAY: *How can you become more like a child before the Lord? Ask and you shall receive!*

DAY 27

Trusting the Mighty One

"Trust in the Lord with all of your heart, and lean not on your own understanding. In all your ways acknowledge him and He will make your paths straight." (Proverbs 3:5-7)

Above all else, trust Me fully—press deeply into Me.
As I sing the sweetest of melodies over you.
With each word, healing is released on My wings.
As the cascade of a waterfall, I am washing you clean.
Each ache of the heart is silenced in the soothing salve of My voice.
The hurt has spoken its last reminder of your painful past.
My Word is stronger, My testimony greater than the works of darkness.
In the night, I spoke new life over you—new life has sprung forth.
In the power of My Blood, I have made all things new.
In your death to the flesh, you were resurrected in Me.

I have sealed your life and called you as My own.
I have known who you were to be from the beginning.
Behold, now in My time I have made all things new.
So, trust Me, My beloved, I am yours and you are Mine.
You know the nature of My face and have known My ways.
In My perfect love, I only give good gifts to My children.
I have longed to fulfill your heart in the fullest measure.
I am bringing it to pass, and I ask you once again to trust Me.
Freefall into My love and hold on loosely to the natural world.
I am taking you into the heavens and leaving you there.
Though you dwell in the natural realm, heaven is brought to earth.
Be prepared. Be expectant. Be YOU. Trust in ME.

QUESTION OF THE DAY: *In what ways does trust in God prepare your heart to receive His promises?*

DAY 28

The Day of the Lord

"And afterward, I will pour out my Spirit on all people. Your sons and daughters will prophesy, your old men will dream dreams, your young men will see visions. Even on my servants, both men and women, I will pour out my Spirit in those days. I will show wonders in the heavens and on earth, blood and fire and billows of smoke. The sun will be turned to darkness and the moon to blood before the coming of the great and dreadful day of the Lord. And everyone who calls on the name of the Lord will be saved; for on Mount Zion and in Jerusalem there will be deliverance, as the Lord has said, even among survivors whom the Lord calls." (Joel 2:28-32)

Like a wave of glory in a rush of the tide.
You are healing the hearts of Your people!
A tsunami of Your Spirit is on the rise.
A tidal wave of signs and wonders.
A rushing over and a crying out,
The latter glory is raining down.

To him who sees and does not speak;
To him who dreams and does not seek;
Your time is now—your destiny is going to peak.
God has anointed your feet to take the land.
Now walk. Be bold. Go forth.
Hand in hand.
Seek and you shall find.
Trust and you will see.
Everything He has promised.
It will surely come to be.
Look to the face of our King—His latter story!
Like a wave of glory in a rush of the tide.
You are healing the hearts of Your people!
A tsunami of Your Spirit is on the rise.
A tidal wave of signs and wonders.
A rushing over and a crying out,
The latter glory is raining down.

QUESTION OF THE DAY: *How have you experienced God's glory? Write a note explaining this experience and how it affected your view of who He is.*

DAY 29

Anchor

"We have this hope as an anchor for the soul, firm and secure. It enters the inner sanctuary behind the curtain." (Hebrews 6:19)

"And He was in the hinder part of the ship, asleep on a pillow; and they awoke him, and said to him, 'Master, care you not that we perish?' And He arose and rebuked the wind, and said to the sea, 'Peace, be still.' And the wind ceased, and there was a great calm." (Mark 4:38-4:39)

You are the anchor of my soul,
In You I hope; my soul is made whole.
I have never known a love like You.
All my life, You stood knocking at my door—
The door of my heart, awaiting my reply,
Patiently enduring longsuffering.
Who has a heart like Yours, God?
You are the anchor of my soul.
In You I trust; my heart made whole.

You have brought me to Yourself.
So recklessly devoted am I,
Swept away in the rivers of Your love,
Enamored by Your countenance.
There is nothing like Your touch.
You are the anchor of my soul.
In You I dream; my heart made whole.
You steady my feet in the sea of life,
Carrying me so diligently through every storm.
Though all else shifts and changes,
The movement of the seas will not shake me,
For You are the anchor of my soul.
In You I rest; my life made whole.
As Jesus rested at the helm,
So am I at rest in the helm of Your heart—
From beginning to end,
To the finish and from the start.
For You are the anchor of my soul.
In You I abide; my dreams made whole.

QUESTION OF THE DAY: *How has your faith in Jesus Christ anchored your life? How does He steady your ship in the seas of life?*

DAY 30

Prophetic Word for the Body

"Very truly I tell you, whoever believes in me will do the works I have been doing, and they will do even greater things than these, because I go to the Father." (John 14:12)

The Day is coming. The Day is near. The Day is upon us. The Day is here. Make haste, My beloved! There is an urgency in the Spirit. A move of God is taking the land. Be single-minded in your approach to life. Only the work of God is eternal. Only the move of God will suffice. "Very truly I tell you, the Son can do nothing by himself; he can do only what he sees his Father doing, because whatever the Father does the Son does also" (John 5:19). As My sons and daughters, you are to move in union with the Father. The works of the flesh will not suffice. Make haste, beloved! Get ready to move by the winds of the Spirit. Things are shifting and changing, for I am doing a new thing on the earth and calling My people home to Me. Run into the Father's house and know that He welcomes you with open arms.

Jeremiah 33:3: "Call upon me and I will answer you and show you great and mighty things which you did not know!" This is a promise. Do not fall into doubt. Believe in the word I have given you!

"Then you will call on me and come and pray to me, and I will listen to you" (Jeremiah 29:12). It is important that you keep close to Me, beloved! You know My voice, I hear you call. I will answer and watch as My Spirit unfolds it all!

We are in the union of marriage! I have vowed myself to you eternally. You are learning My ways, My nature, My patterns, and My face. You are experiencing the incredible and immeasurable depths of My love for you. My love and our relationship will fuel you in the days to come! It is the only source of life. Everything comes from the overflow of our time. So sit with Me! Be with Me! For in the days to come, even the elect will be deceived. It is important to stay close to Me and see as I am seeing. You have the mind of Christ!

Do not fear! I am in the business of restoring souls and redeeming the lives of My faithful ones! My remnant bride is fully Mine! I have claimed her and am making a way for her on the Holy Road of Purity! So come, and be with Me! Let Me lavish My love upon you. And watch as I work through you!

QUESTION OF THE DAY: *In what ways do you think God is waiting for you to call on Him?*

DAY 31

Prophetic Worship: Good Morning, Beautiful

I don't come to You this morning with an agenda. With questions, petitions, or reasons except for my love for You. My only question for You this morning, my petition is to hear how You are doing. How is Your heart today, God? How is Your heart today, my God? What are You thinking? What are You doing? How are You? What is going on in Heaven today? What are You up to? I want to hear the heartbeat of Heaven. I want to hear the heartbeat of Heaven.

I am just coming to You out of love and relationship. I don't have any questions aside from knowing how You are doing. What are You thinking? How are You feeling? What's going on in Heaven today? For I am so in love with You. And You are more than I could ever ask for. Yes, You are more than I could ever hope for. And so, as I come to You to sing a song and lay it at Your feet, I have one question for You, and that is all that I bring: How's Your heart, God? I want to know. How's Your heart, God? I have to know! And that's all I bring to You in a package of my love; how is Your heart, God? What are You thinking? What are You saying? What are You feeling in Heaven today? I want to know because I love You, God. And just like a lover should, I care about what You think. More than anything. I put You before me. It's for Your glory. The heartbeat of Heaven is beating in me. The heartbeat of Heaven is beating in me.

Today, I don't come with an agenda. I come just to be with You, to know You, and be known by You. That my heart, all of my heart, would align with Yours, God. And I sing a pure song of Spirit and truth and send it up to You in Your throne room saying, what are You thinking, what are You saying, how are You feeling, and what are You doing in Heaven today? Cause I have got to know Your face. I have got to know Your face. How I long to know You, God. Yes, I've got to know Your face.

Good morning, beauty-full. How was Your night? Mine was wonderful with You by my side. As I opened my eyes to see Your sweet face, it was a good morning, a beautiful day. It's a good morning, a beautiful day.

Question of the Day: Tell God how much you care about Him and His heart in a short letter and then ask Him the question, "How is your heart, God?" Write down what you hear.

DAY 32

His Shalom Peace

"*Again, the kingdom of heaven is like a merchant seeking beautiful pearls, who, when he has found one pearl of great price, went and sold all that he had and bought it.*" (Matthew 13:45-46)

"*And He shall be their Peace.*" (Micah 5:5)

How can it be?
My Beloved is such a beautiful picture of WHO Love should be!
What words to describe?
Someone unfathomable; unquantifiable; altogether perfect.
Yet You are waiting upon me?
How can this Lover be?!
I have to know You!
Show me Your face, God!
Every detail, every crevice—
My heart burns for the deepest knowing of who You are.

It is worth it.
It is worth everything.
Greater than anything I could measure.
Any price I could pay.
Allow Your goodness to pass before me!
Though I am unworthy, You have made a way for me.
For I am in Your love!
Soaking in this river of holiness.
It is washing me clean and transforming me from the inside.
I am swept away in the waves of His beauty.
Carried off into the heavens.
Hold me, My Beloved.
Quiet me with Your love.
For I am Yours and You are mine.
What serenity.
What divinity.
A life-giving waterfall.
His complete Shalom Peace.

QUESTION OF THE DAY: *How has God given you peace in your life? In what ways do you choose His peace?*

In Closing

God is everything and immeasurably more than we could comprehend or ask for. In Him is the fulfillment of all things. Thank you for going on this journey with us. Traveling within my heart and the interlacing heart of God; thank you for exploring our intimate connection. My prayer is that this leads to the Spirit- filled discovery and deepening of your own captivating love story with Him. I know this to be the heart of the Father. He yearns for us as a lover and desires that we know Him, are known by Him, and pursue Him in all things.

Let me assure you that you will not be disappointed. There is nothing else like Him. It brings me to tears to think about the sweetness and priceless relationship with God we are given the opportunity to have on this earth and into eternity. He is the fulfillment of all things; He is in all things. "Through Him all things were made; without Him nothing was made that has been made" (John 1:3). So I urge you to look at the source. The source of all life. Do not get caught up in the details of man's agenda or the superficial realities that will pass away with the world. "For, 'all people are like grass, and all their glory is like the flowers of the field; the grass withers and the flowers fall, but the word of the Lord endures forever.' And this is the word that was preached to you" (1 Peter 1:24-25). He is the way, the truth, and the life. His glory will sustain us for eternity. It is such a comforting thought, to know God and be a child of the Creator of the Universe. Redeemed by the precious blood of Jesus. He has called us His own. Marked us and sealed us by His Spirit!

It is our soul's desire to know and be known by God. Everything else comes from the outpouring and overflowing of this relationship. I thank God for you and your time with Him in the secret place and your abiding in Him. I thank You, Lord, for an impartation of passionate romance in relationship with You! That we are all filled to the brim with a knowing of Your love and desire toward us. You loved us first. And now in Your goodness, You have reconciled us to Yourself through the Blood of Yeshua, that we would have eternity to love you back. "'Love the Lord your God with all your heart and with all your soul and with all your strength and with all your mind'; and, 'Love your neighbor as yourself'"" (Luke 10:27). God bless you!

LEAH STARR HARRIS is a dedicated follower of Jesus Christ and a devoted wife and mother of three. Leah is passionate about worship and intimacy with God. She has a story of restoration in Yeshua and knows His beauty and kindness firsthand. She is also a professional counselor in the state of Texas and loves to read, write, dance, and sing.

Made in the USA
Columbia, SC
05 April 2025